To

From

Date

There is no sight on earth
more appealing than the sight
of a woman making
dinner for someone
she loves.

— Thomas Wolfe

The Dowry Cookbook

A personal collection of your most treasured recipes

Created by
Cynthia Salvato

Cynthia Salvato is a Certified Executive Pastry Chef who teaches pastry arts at The International Baking and Pastry Institute at Johnson and Wales University in Providence, Rhode Island, and is the President of the Dowry Cookie Company.

To order additional copies of this book or for information about Dowry Cookies, write:
The Dowry Cookie Company • P.O. Box 25091 • Providence, RI 02905

A portion of the proceeds from the sale of this book will fund a scholarship for single mothers.

Special thanks from the author go to **Linda Beaulieu***, whose endless support, knowledge and friendship helped to make this project a reality;* **Lars Johannson***, whose wisdom, guidance and example will transcend a lifetime;* **Natalie Manning***, graphic designer extraorinaire, whose artistic talents made the Dowry Cookie Company even more special; and all the people at* **Favorite Recipes Press** *for their enthusiasm and for making a dream come true..*

ISBN: 0-9654328-0-7

Designed, edited and published under the direction of:
FRP™
P.O. 305142 • Nashville, TN 37230 • 1-800-358-0560

Managing Editor	Mary Cummings
Project Manager	Jane Hinshaw
Book & Cover Design	Brad Whitfield
Photograph Colorist	Betty Gilpin
Art Director	Steve Newman
Typography & Design	Susan Breining
Production Manager	Mark Sloan

Manufactured in the United States of America
First Printing: 1996

This book is dedicated to
my grandmothers,
Anna Salvato (Noni)
&
Mary Theresa Pineault (Nanna).
Thanks for all the memories
and good food.

In Sicily, a dowry cookbook is a collection of treasured recipes that a girl inherits from her family as part of the portion that she brings to her marriage, along with table linens, dishware and the other necessities of housekeeping. The cookbooks are a way of preserving a family's heritage and memories along with its most beloved recipes. Antique dealers throughout Italy value them as much for the way of life that they preserve as for the forgotten recipes.

I discovered dowry cookbooks when I delved into my family background when I founded the Dowry Cookie Company in 1995 in Rhode Island. It began when my aunt Lucille gave me a recipe for Cantuccini, which is a cookie our family has been enjoying for years. It became a favorite in a line of renaissance cookies that formed the basis for the cookie company and stimulated my interest in family recipes and heritage.

For fifteen years I had enjoyed travelling to the homelands of my grandparents. During these visits, I was able to trace many of my family's favorite dishes. I discovered that the women in my family are wonderful cooks. My father's family, from the beautiful island of Sicily, had feasted me with dinners featuring eggplant parmesan, seafood, braciola, pasta and many others. My mother's family came from Newfoundland and Prince Edward Island, where I learned to appreciate dishes like pork pie, any kind of potato, boiled dinners and peas pudding, an old Newfie specialty.

In Newfoundland, my great aunt Rita still cooks on her wood stove, which takes center stage in the kitchen of her home that looks out over beautiful Conception Bay. I can still taste the wonderful loaves of bread that we ate hot from that oven.

My aunt Nancy, who lives in the Boston area, still prepares Baduni, a Sicilian dish, on a beautiful enamel stove that has been part of her family's kitchen for over forty years. Without that stove, Thanksgiving meals would not be the same.

When I was designing the logo for the Dowry Cookie Company, my family and I pored over old photographs of relatives who were married during the early 1900s.

I knew that we had found a treasure when we came across Graziella's wedding photograph. Much to my surprise, Graziella, who is my father's cousin, is alive and well and living in Sicily with her family. Without hesitation, she gave me her permission to use the photograph to adorn the cookie packages. Her haunting beauty has since prompted a sort of love affair between her and my customers. Since Graziella has also passed along to me the recipes that she and her daughters have enjoyed for years, she seems to personify the spirit of the dowry cookbook, so we knew that she was the perfect choice for the cover of this book.

I have included in this book, as my gift to you, a number of my most treasured family recipes. I hope that they will encourage you to begin a dowry cookbook for yourself or someone you love.

A tutti i buongustai. Buon appetito!
To all gourmets. Good eating!

"Of soup and love, the first is best."
A Dowry Cookbook is both.

Build a Library of Family Recipes

Grandmothers, mothers and aunts can begin to collect family memories and recipes for a girl very early in her life and make it an ongoing project to present to her when she marries or leaves home. There can be no more special gift than the one that reminds her of the good memories and good food that nurtured her and her family for generations before her. Even those of you who have been married or away from home for years can enjoy collecting these recipes from family members who may be growing old.

Bridal Shower or Wedding Gift

A Dowry Cookbook can be compiled all at once by the friends and family of the bride who has not been collecting family recipes over the years. The recipes can be collected in advance and brought to a bridal shower, or guests can bring a recipe to the shower to add to the Dowry Cookbook. For brides who don't have time for showers, the enterprising friend or relative can make it her project to collect the recipes as a wedding gift.

Baby Shower

Even though the need may seem light years away, a Dowry Cookbook can establish the theme for a baby shower and form the nucleus for a treasured collection of recipes and memories. Remember to save some blank pages for the girl to fill in as she grows up.

To Collect the Recipes

There is a page in the back of the book that can be cut out and copied or simply copied to give to relatives, friends or shower guests. There is a recipe on the back to serve as a guide for writing the recipe. When the recipes are collected, the person who has made this her project can copy them or have them copied into the book. If there are particularly treasured handwritten recipes, they can be spraymounted on the page instead of copied, along with photographs where available. Several double pages are provided in the book for exceptionally long recipes. You may even want a separate book for each category of recipes.

RECIPE

Pollo Spezzato

Fondest memories from Lucy Lentine. My cousin Lucy is a terrific cook with an infectious sense of humor and a huge heart. I was pleasantly surprised that she chose our family favorite for this book. I learned that we all make it a little differently, but we all love it just as much.

1 chicken, cut into pieces
Olive oil
1 large onion, chopped
3 large cloves of garlic, finely chopped
2 tablespoons dried oregano
2 tablespoons chopped parsley
Salt and pepper to taste
1/2 cup water
1 pound thin linguini or spaghetti

Rinse the chicken and pat dry. Sauté in the olive oil in a skillet until golden brown on all sides.
Add the onion and garlic and sauté until tender.
Sprinkle with the oregano, parsley, salt and pepper. Add the water and cover tightly.
Simmer for 30 minutes. Remove the chicken from the skillet.
Cook the pasta and transfer it to a serving bowl. Pour the cooking sauce over the pasta, and toss to mix well. Spoon onto serving plates and add the chicken.
Top with freshly grated cheese.
Serves four.

What is paradise but a garden, an orchard of trees and herbs full of pleasure.
— William Lawson

RECIPE

Fondest memories from

If I can't have too many truffles, I'll do without truffles.
— Colette

RECIPE

Fondest memories from

Life is like an onion. You peel it off one layer at a time and sometimes you weep.

— Carl Sandburg

RECIPE

Fondest memories from

The destiny of nations depends on what they eat.

— Brillat-Savarin

RECIPE

Fondest memories from

There is no love sincerer than the love of food.

— George Bernard Shaw

Faithful God,

let this table be a sign of tomorrow's hope already here, when with the world which hungers for your justice and peace, we shall come together singing your name as our very own.

Parrot Tulip

— *Father John Giuliani*

The Benedictine Grange
West Redding Connecticut

RECIPE

Fondest memories from

How can you be expected to govern a country that has 246 kinds of cheese?

— Charles de Gaulle

RECIPE

Fondest memories from

***B**read deals with living things, with giving things, with growth, with the seed, the grains that nurture…*

...It is not coincidence that we say bread is the staff of life.

— Lionel Piolane

RECIPE

Fondest memories from

Food is an important part of a balanced diet.

— Fran Lebowitz

RECIPE

Spaghetti Foriana

Fondest memories from Mom and Dad. As a child I loved to vacation with my family on Cape Cod. We always ventured to Provincetown to dine at Ciro's and Sal's for my father's favorite dish. At the time they would not give him the recipe, so my dad tenaciously worked to duplicate it. Mom insists on using thin pasta, because "thick pasta just doesn't cut it." This recipe can be made the day before; simply warm the sauce before serving and toss in the pasta.

5 cloves of garlic, minced
4 to 5 inches anchovy paste from the tube
3/4 cup olive oil
1/2 cup coarsely chopped walnuts
1/3 cup pine nuts, lightly toasted
1/2 cup dark raisins
5 tablespoons chopped fresh parsley
1/8 teaspoon crushed red pepper
Black pepper to taste
1 pound thin spaghetti

Sauté the garlic and anchovy paste in the heated olive oil in a heavy skillet over low heat for 3 to 4 minutes, stirring with a wooden spoon; do not burn the garlic. Add the walnuts, pine nuts, raisins, parsley, red pepper and black pepper. Simmer for 4 to 5 minutes. Cook the pasta and transfer it into a serving bowl. Add the Foriana and toss to coat well. Serve with grated Parmesan cheese. Serves four.

Cooking is like love — it should be entered into with abandon or not at all.

— Harriet Van Horne

RECIPE

Fondest memories from

Only the pure of heart can make a good soup.

— Ludwig van Beethoven

RECIPE

Fondest memories from

As for rosemary, I let it run all over my garden walls, not only because my bees love it but because it is the herb sacred to remembrance and to friendship.

— Sir Thomas More

RECIPE

Fondest memories from

A loaf of bread, a jug of wine and thou...

— Edward Fitzgerald,
The Rubaiyat of Omar Khayyam

RECIPE

Fondest memories from

Come unto me all you whose stomachs are aching, and I will restore you.

— Sign outside the first restaurant in France, 1765

Father,

bless this food which re-creates our bodies. May hearing of your word re-create our souls.

— Mount St. Mary's Abbey

Wrentham, Massachusetts

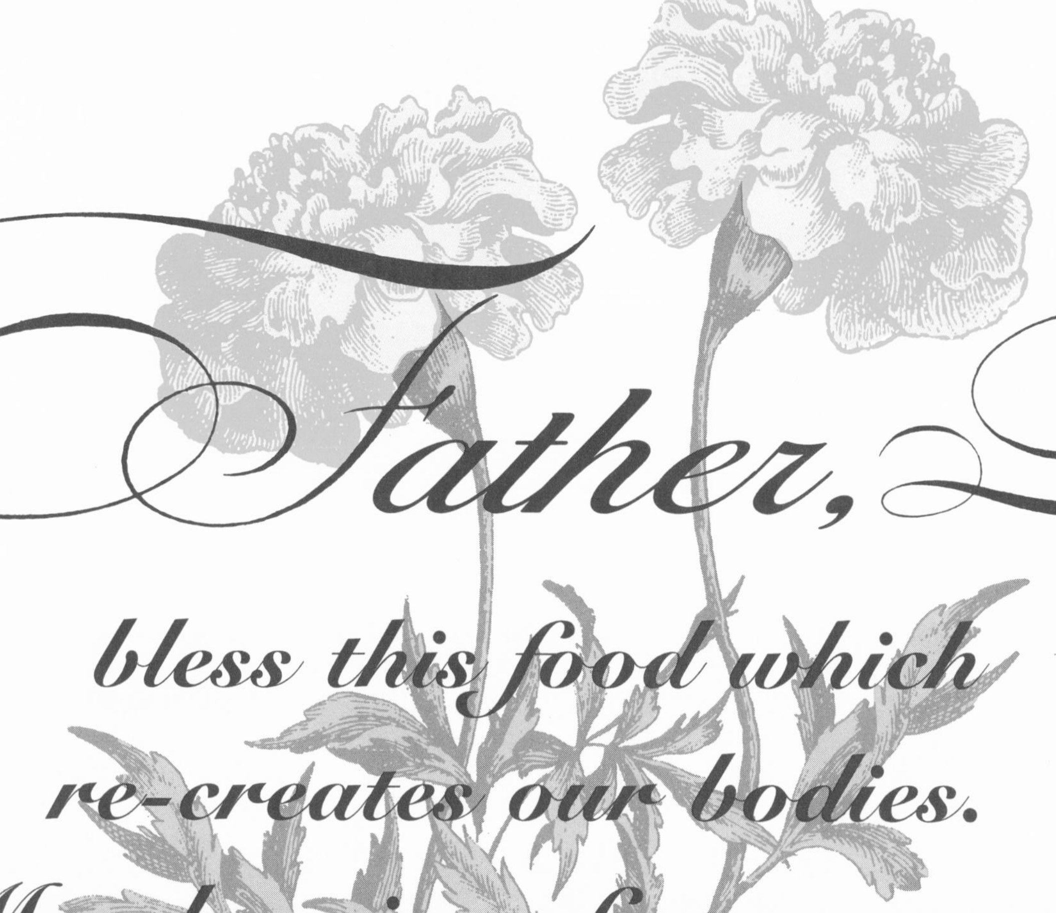

Double French Marigold

RECIPE

Fondest memories from

Romance is the icing but love is the cake.

— Unknown

RECIPE

Fondest memories from

"But wait a bit," the Oyster cried, "before we have a chat.
For some of us are out of breath, and all of us are fat."

— Lewis Carroll

RECIPE

Fondest memories from

Cheese: Milk's leap towards immortality.

— Clifton Fadiman

RECIPE

Arancini

Fondest memories from Mom. Christmas was always an event at my parents' house and people came from everywhere to celebrate. The first signs of holiday preparation began about three weeks before Christmas with the fruitcake project, with mountains of candied fruits, nuts and butter on the table and Mom in the pantry greasing everything from tube pans to coffee cans to bake in. Cookies and more cookies followed the fruitcake festival. She hid them so there would be some left for Christmas, but we always found them. Mom then went on to prepare lasagna, antipasto, stuffed mushrooms and artichokes, as well as the usual turkey with all the fixings. One of our favorite dishes was Arancini, named because it resembled the orange in size and shape. She insists that you must use homemade chicken broth, but in a pinch, you can get away with canned.

And the best bread was of my mother's own making — the best in all the land!

— Sir Henry James

Arancini

3 cups uncooked arborio rice
2 quarts homemade chicken broth
1 cup grated Parmesan cheese
2 large eggs, slightly beaten
1/2 pound ground top round
1 tablespoon olive oil
1/4 cup tomato sauce
Salt and pepper to taste
8 to 12 ounces mozzarella cheese, cut into 1/2-inch cubes
3 or 4 eggs, beaten
Italian bread crumbs or cornmeal
Vegetable oil for frying

Cook the rice in the chicken broth in a heavy saucepan, using the package directions; stir frequently to prevent burning. Remove from the heat. Stir in the Parmesan cheese and 2 eggs quickly. Cool completely and chill overnight. Sauté the ground round in the olive oil in a heavy skillet. Stir in the tomato sauce, salt and pepper.
Cook until thickened; mixture should not be soupy. Cool completely.
Scoop out the rice by 3/4 cupfuls. Place in the hand and make a well in the center.
Fill with the meat mixture or a cube of cheese and shape into a ball, enclosing the filling completely.
Dip into the beaten eggs and coat with the bread crumbs.
Fill a heavy skillet half full with vegetable oil and heat to 350 degrees.
Cook the arancini in the heated oil until golden brown on all sides.
Drain on paper towels. Serve warm. Makes eight to ten arancini.

No mean woman can cook well, for it calls for a light head, a generous spirit, and a large heart.

— Paul Gauguin

RECIPE

Fondest memories from

If I had to choose just one plant for the garden,
I should be content with basil.

— Elizabeth David

RECIPE

Fondest memories from

Do that in less time than it takes to cook asparagus.
— A Roman expression

RECIPE

Fondest memories from

Looks can be deceiving — it's eating that's believing.
—James Thurber

Had I but one penny in the world, thou shouldst have it for gingerbread.
— William Shakespeare

For each new morning with its light, for rest and shelter of the night, or health and food, for love and friends or everything thy goodness sends.

— Ralph Waldo Emerson

Double Violet

RECIPE

Fondest memories from

A man taking basil from a woman will love her always.

— Sir Thomas More

RECIPE

Fondest memories from

Don't let love interfere with your appetite. It never does with mine.

— Anthony Trollope

RECIPE

Fondest memories from

Garlic is after all one of the major food groups.
— Cynthia Salvato

RECIPE

Fondest memories from

I stick to asparagus which still seems to inspire gentle thought.

— Charles Lamb

RECIPE

Involtini di Pesca Spada (Rolled Swordfish)

Fondest memories from Josephine Alibrandi. I first met my cousin Josephine during the development stages of the Dowry Cookie Company and credit much of the company's character to her assistance. I have a fond memory of a family dinner party at her house, an evening of food and conversation that would be hard to duplicate. Josephine lived in Sicily for many years and has a passion for Old World Sicilian-style dishes, which usually include fish, like this family recipe. The sauce, Salmora, is great with just about anything.

Swordfish

10 slices fresh Italian bread
2 tablespoons chopped fresh parsley
2 tablespoons grated Parmesan cheese
20 to 30 capers
20 to 30 green olives, chopped
1/2 teaspoon garlic powder or garlic salt
1/4 cup (about) olive oil
32 slices of swordfish, 4 to 5 inches long and 1/4 inch thick

Salmora

1 cup water
1/4 cup olive oil
Juice of 2 lemons
1 teaspoon chopped parsley or oregano
Garlic salt or powder to taste

For the swordfish, process the bread to crumbs in a blender. Transfer to a clean bowl. Add the parsley, cheese, capers, olives, garlic powder and olive oil and mix well. Place the swordfish slices on waxed paper. Spread with the bread crumb mixture and roll to enclose the mixture. Thread 4 rolls on each skewer. Broil for 4 minutes on each side. For the salmora, heat the water and olive oil in a saucepan. Whisk in the lemon juice, parsley and garlic salt. Serve with the swordfish rolls. Serves six, or four Italians.

I saw him even now going the way of all flesh, that is to say towards the kitchen.

— John Webster

RECIPE

Fondest memories from

'Tis not the meat, but 'tis the appetite makes eating a delight.
— Sir John Suckling

RECIPE

Fondest memories from

Too much of a good thing can be wonderful.
— Mae West

RECIPE

Fondest memories from

There is no such thing as a little garlic.
— Arthur Baer

RECIPE

Fondest memories from

Garlic is the ketchup of intellectuals.
— Anonymous

Food

God's love made edible,
may we be swept into
your presence.

— Brother Thomas
Nada Hermitage, Crefstone, Colorado

RECIPE

Fondest memories from

Cauliflower is nothing but cabbage with a college education.

— Mark Twain

RECIPE

Fondest memories from

Without bread, everyone is an orphan.
— Italian expression

RECIPE

Fondest memories from

What are we having with bread?
— Italian expression

RECIPE

Fondest memories from

Give me books, fruit, French wine and fine weather, and a little music out of doors, played by someone I do not know.

— John Keats

Boursin Potatoes

Fondest memories from Nancie Coogan. My sister Nancie's passion for cooking developed as a child. Every Wednesday night after religion class, she would walk over to my grandmother's house, and they would have a cooking lesson where Nancie learned some of my grandmother's cooking secrets. I hope that some day she will share them with me. In the meantime, she has given me this modern-day recipe which we all enjoy during the holidays.

1 (5-ounce) package Boursin cheese
1 pint heavy cream
3 pounds unpeeled red potatoes, thinly sliced
3 tablespoons chopped Italian parsley

Melt the cheese in the cream in a nonreactive saucepan over low heat, stirring to blend well. Arrange half the potatoes in overlapping layers in a buttered 9x13-inch baking dish. Spoon half the sauce over the top. Repeat the layers with the remaining potatoes and cheese sauce. Sprinkle with the parsley. Bake at 400 degrees for 1 hour. Serve immediately. Serves six to eight.

If beef's the king of meat, potato's the queen of the garden world.
— Irish proverb

RECIPE

Fondest memories from

There is an emanation from the heart in genuine hospitality which cannot be described but is immediately felt,

...and puts the stranger at once at ease.

— Washington Irving

God,
bless this food we are
about to receive.
Give bread to those who hunger,
and hunger for justice
who have bread.

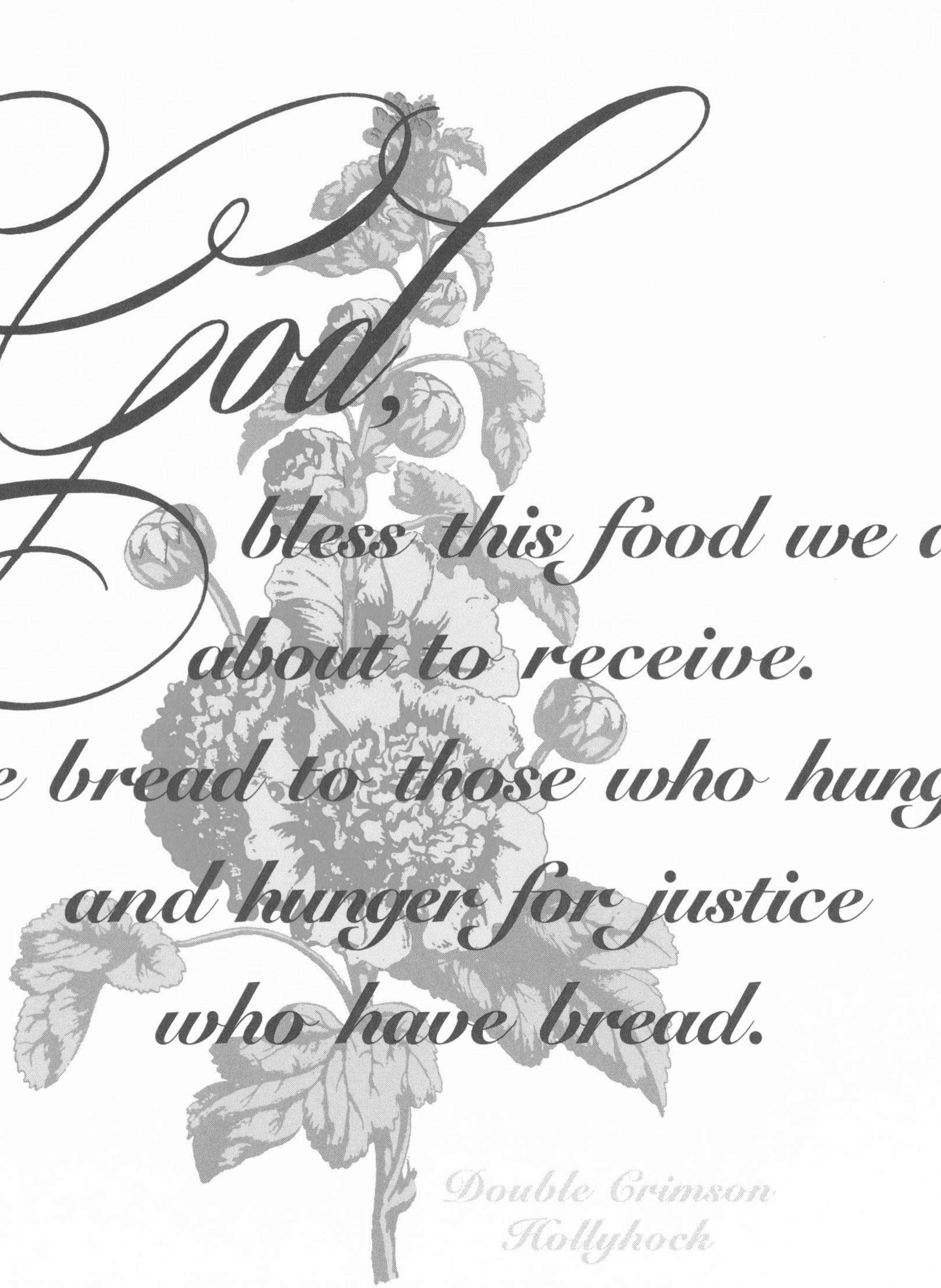

Double Crimson
Hollyhock

RECIPE

Fondest memories from

Roast beef medium is not a food. It is a philosophy.

— Edna Ferber

RECIPE

Fondest memories from

I'd rather have roses at my table than diamonds on my neck.

— Emma Goldman

RECIPE

Fondest memories from

Man does not live by bread alone but by every word of God.

— Deuteronomy 8:3

RECIPE

Fondest memories from

The best things in life aren't things.
— Art Buchwald

RECIPE

Bleu Cheese Cheesecake

Fondest memories from Lora Brody, a prolific cookbook author whose love of food is just as exciting as her love of life. From her personal recipe file comes this exciting hors d'oeuvre, which will be a hit at your next dinner party. It requires an eight-inch cheesecake pan that is three inches deep. This is not a springform pan and can be found in kitchen shops.

1/3 cup fine bread crumbs
7 tablespoons freshly grated Parmesan cheese
1 medium onion, finely chopped
3 tablespoons butter
8 ounces bleu cheese, Roquefort or Stilton, crumbled
28 ounces cream cheese, softened
4 extra-large eggs
1/3 cup heavy cream
1/2 pound lean bacon, crisp-fried, crumbled
Several drops of Tabasco sauce
Freshly ground pepper to taste

Line the bottom of the cheesecake pan with buttered baking parchment or waxed paper. Coat with a mixture of the bread crumbs and Parmesan cheese, shaking out the excess. Sauté the onion in the butter in a saucepan. Process the bleu cheese, cream cheese, eggs and heavy cream in a food processor for 30 seconds. Add the onion, acon, Tabasco sauce and pepper. Spoon into the prepared pan, smooth the top and bang the pan on the counter top to release air bubbles. Place into a baking pan large enough that the sides do not touch and place on the center rack of an oven preheated to 300 degrees. Add enough hot water to the larger pan to reach halfway up the side of the cheesecake pan. Bake for 1 hour and 40 minutes, adding water if necessary. Turn the oven off, leaving the cheesecake in the closed oven for 1 hour longer. Let stand until completely cool. Place plastic wrap and a plate on the cheesecake pan and invert, shaking or banging on the counter if necessary to remove. Remove the parchment and invert again onto a serving plate. Serves six.

Life itself is the proper binge.
— Julia Child

RECIPE

Fondest memories from

Let them eat cake.
— Marie Antoinette

RECIPE

Fondest memories from

It's no use boiling your cabbage twice.
— Irish proverb

RECIPE

Fondest memories from

Parsley — the jewel of herbs, both in the pot and on the plate.

— Unknown

RECIPE

Banana Bread

Fondest memories from Denise Fleming and Mary Theresa Pineault. My sister Denise's favorite hobby is cooking, and one wall of her kitchen is filled with cookbooks and magazines. I had completely forgotten about this recipe for banana bread from my grandmother that Denise makes for her children almost daily. It brings back fond memories of my grandmother, and I was glad to know that yet another generation is enjoying it.

1/2 cup shortening
1 cup sugar
2 cups flour
2 extra-large eggs
1 teaspoon baking powder
1 teaspoon baking soda
1/2 teaspoon salt
3 very ripe bananas, beaten

Cream the shortening and sugar with 1 tablespoon of the flour at medium speed in a mixer bowl until light and fluffy. Beat in the eggs 1 at a time. Sift the remaining flour with the baking powder, baking soda and salt. Add to the creamed mixture alternately with the bananas, mixing well after each addition. Spoon into a greased and floured 4x9-inch loaf pan. Bake at 350 degrees for 1 hour. You may also bake it in 12 muffin cups for 20 minutes. Serves twelve.

I'm glad you met me.

— Wilfred Pineault
Engraved on the headstone of my grandparents

RECIPE

Fondest memories from

Who can find a virtuous woman? For her price is far above rubies,

... The heart of her husband doth safely trust in her.

— Proverbs 31:10-11

RECIPE

Fondest memories from

All the days of the oppressed are wretched, but the cheerful heart has a continual feast.

— Proverbs 15:15

RECIPE

Fondest memories from

In the restaurant of life you get what you order.
— Unknown

O thou who clothes the lilies,
Who feeds the birds of the sky,
Who leads the lambs to pasture,
And the deer to the waterside,
Who multiplied the loaves and fishes,
And changes the water to wine,
Do thou come to our table as giver
and as our guest to dine.

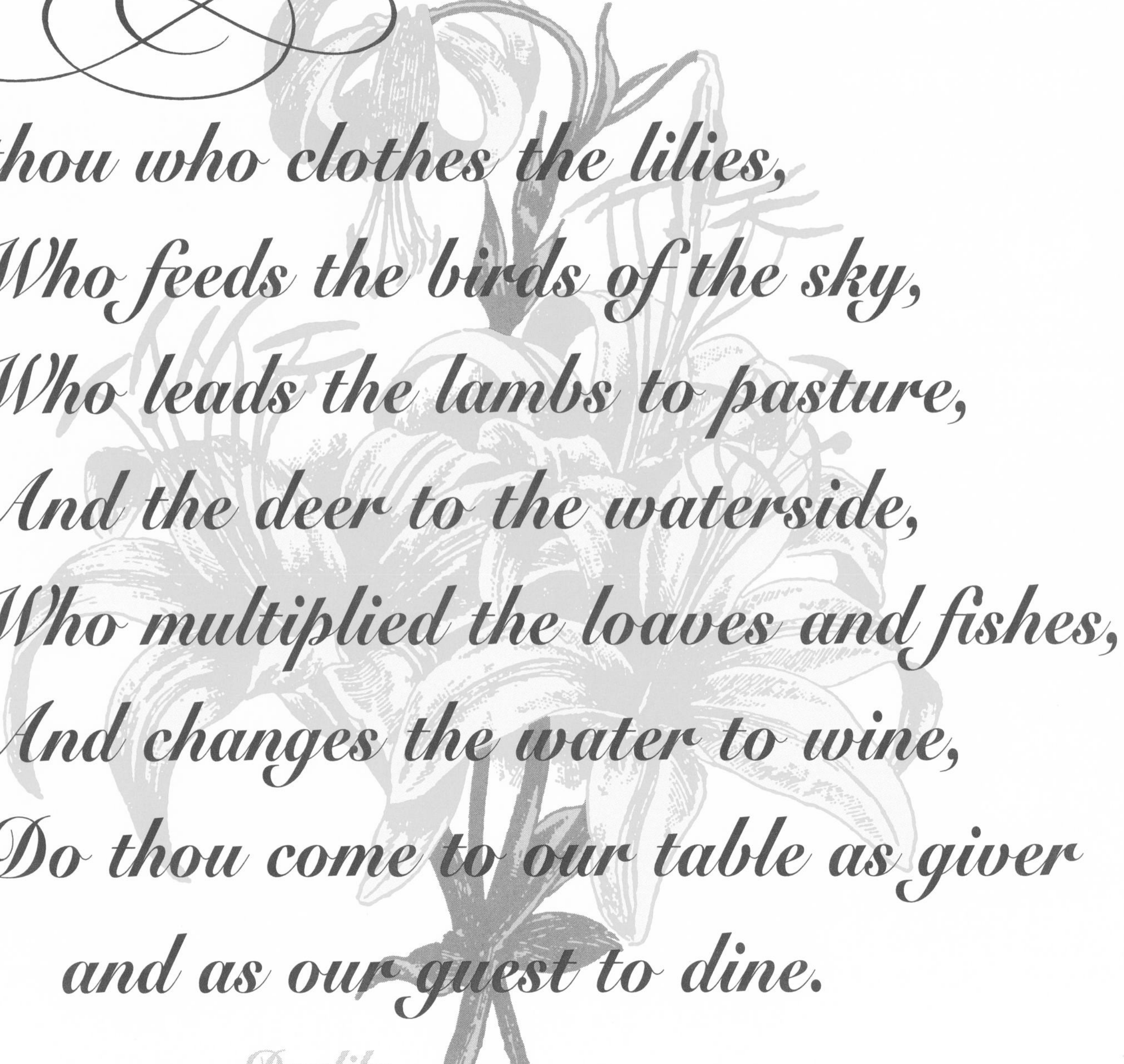

Daylily

RECIPE

Fondest memories from

Blessed are those who hunger and thirst for righteousness, for they will be filled.

— Matthew 5:6

RECIPE

Fondest memories from

Eat no onions nor garlic, for we are to utter sweet breath.
— William Shakespeare

RECIPE

Fondest memories from

To the table or to bed you must come when you are bid.

— Laura Esquivel

RECIPE

Fondest memories from

An army marches on its stomach.
— Napoleon Bonaparte

RECIPE

Zuppa di Polpette (Meatball Soup)

Fondest memories from Lucille Salvato. Memories of family meals always begin in the kitchen of my aunt Lucille's house where, on any given day, you can catch her baking the world's best apple pie. During Thanksgiving she prepares this soup, which is everyone's favorite. It would not be Thanksgiving without it.

1 small chicken, cut up
1 large onion, cut into quarters
2 carrots, thinly sliced
1 medium tomato, cut into halves
1 rib celery, chopped
Pinch of turmeric for color
1/2 teaspoon thyme
Salt and pepper to taste
1 pound lean ground beef
1 cup fresh bread crumbs
1 tablespoon chopped fresh parsley
1 large egg
1/3 cup grated Romano cheese
1 1/2 to 2 cups soup pasta, cooked, drained

Rinse the chicken well. Combine with the onion, carrots, tomato, celery, turmeric, thyme, salt, pepper and enough water to cover by 4 to 5 inches in an 8-quart stockpot. Cook for 1 1/2 hours. Remove the chicken and vegetables. Cut up some of the chicken and add it to the soup if you like, or reserve for another use. Process the vegetables in a food mill and return to the stock. Combine the ground beef, bread crumbs, parsley, egg, cheese and salt and pepper to taste in a stainless steel bowl and mix well. Shape by tablespoonfuls into small balls. Add to the stock. Simmer for 30 minutes. Spoon the pasta into the serving bowls. Ladle the soup into the bowls. Serve with additional grated Romano cheese. Serves six to eight.

Soup, it breathes reassurance, it offers consolation; after a weary day it promotes sociability.

— Louis P. DeGouy

RECIPE

Fondest memories from

Strange to see how a good dinner and feasting reconciles everybody.

— Samuel Pepys

RECIPE

Fondest memories from

No man is lonely eating spaghetti; it requires so much attention.

— Christopher Morley

RECIPE

Fondest memories from

Part of the secret of success in life is to eat what you like and let the food fight it out inside.

— Mark Twain

Life, within doors, has few pleasanter aspects than a neatly arranged and well-provisioned breakfast table.

— Nathaniel Hawthorne

*Eat your bread with joy
and drink with a merry heart,
because it is now that God
favors your work.*

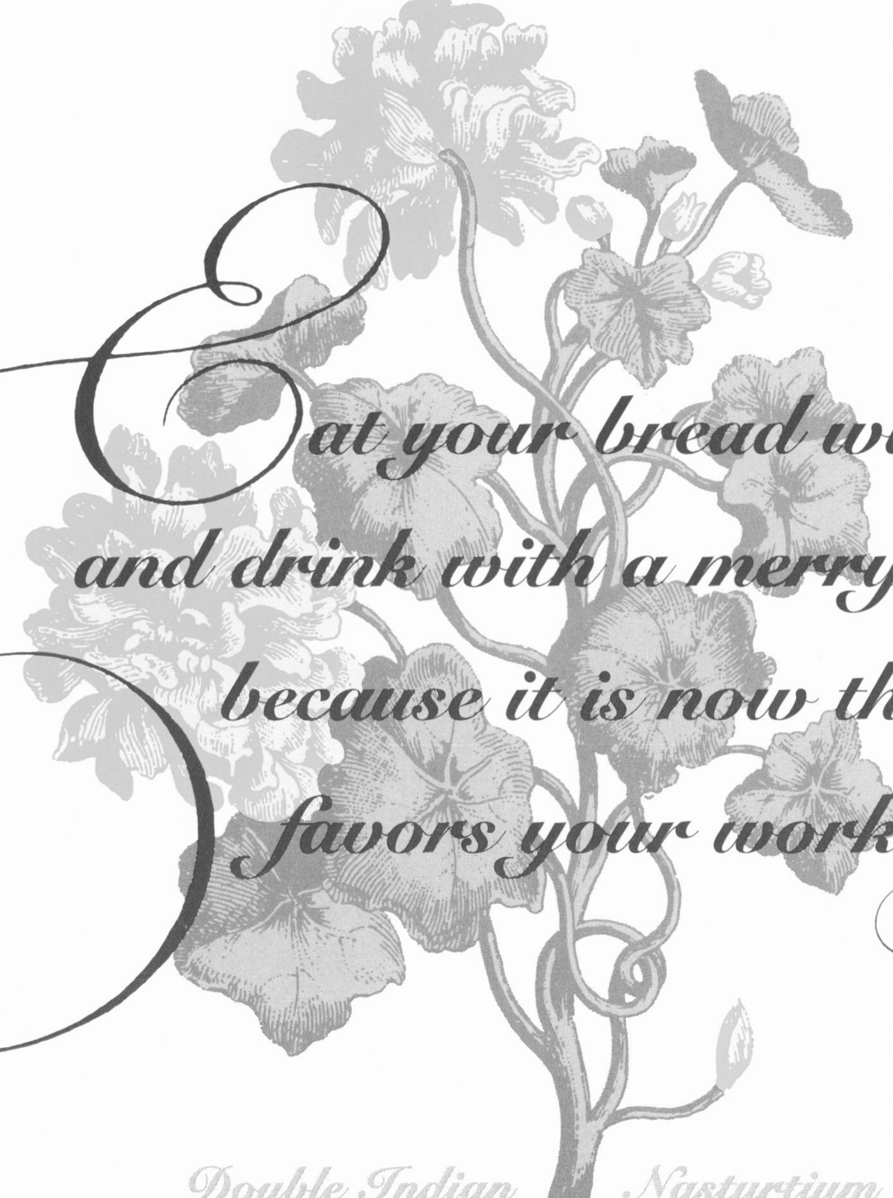

Double Indian Nasturtium

RECIPE

Fondest memories from

Tell me what you eat and I will tell you what you are.

— Brillat-Savarin

RECIPE

Fondest memories from

He was a bold man that first ate an oyster.
— Jonathan Swift

RECIPE

Fondest memories from

As for butter versus margarine, I trust cows more than chemists.
— Joan Gussow

RECIPE

Fondest memories from

The first thing I remember liking that liked me back was food.

— Rhoda Morgenstern

Coeur de Crème

Fondest memories from Cynthia Salvato. Valentine's Day is without a doubt my favorite holiday. I call it the Super Bowl for women. Once a year during a "Super Bowl" a group of us get together and feast on this luscious renaissance dessert. Serve this to your Valentine, with fresh red raspberries and champagne. It's all you'll need!

8 ounces cream cheese, softened
1 cup sugar
1/4 cup sour cream
2 tablespoons Grand Marnier or Triple Sec
1 cup heavy cream
1 pint fresh raspberries

Use a ceramic heart-shaped Coeur de Crème mold with drainage holes in the bottom.
Line the mold with 2 layers of cheesecloth.
Beat the cream cheese and sugar at medium speed in a mixer bowl until smooth.
Mix in the sour cream and Grand Marnier. Transfer to a clean bowl.
Beat the heavy cream in a mixer bowl until medium peaks form. Fold into the cream cheese mixture.
Spoon into the prepared mold and smooth the surface. Cover with another layer of cheesecloth.
Place on a tray to catch the moisture that will drain. Chill for 8 hours or longer.
Remove the cheesecloth on the top and unmold the dessert onto a serving plate.
Serve with fresh raspberries.
Serves four to six.

Life is uncertain...eat dessert first.
— Unknown

RECIPE

Fondest memories from

An idealist is one who, on noticing that a rose smells better than a cabbage, concludes that it will also make a better soup.

— H. L. Mencken

RECIPE

Fondest memories from

To eat is human, to digest, divine.

— Mark Twain

RECIPE

Fondest memories from

The way to a man's heart is through his stomach.

—Fanny Fern

RECIPE

Linzer Torte

Fondest memories from Jaime Nero. In Scandinavian countries, when a man wanted to propose marriage, he brought a Linzer Torte to the home of the woman's parents. If they ate the torte, the proposal was accepted, and if she threw it into the street, well, need I say more? On Saturday nights you may find my good friend and neighbor Jaime and me waiting for a Linzer Torte delivery.

1 cup unsalted butter, softened
1/3 cup sugar
3 egg yolks
1 3/4 cups flour
1 cup ground almonds
1/4 teaspoon cinnamon
1/4 teaspoon mace
1/2 teaspoon vanilla extract
1 (12-ounce) jar raspberry preserves
1 tablespoon raspberry brandy
2 tablespoons confectioners' sugar

Cream the butter and sugar in a mixer bowl until light and fluffy. Add the egg yolks alternately with the flour and almonds, mixing well after each addition. Mix in the cinnamon, mace and vanilla. Spread 1/4 inch thick in a greased and floured 10-inch tart pan with removable bottom; reserve the excess dough. Mix the preserves, brandy and confectioners' sugar in a bowl. Spread in the prepared pan. Roll the remaining dough into 8 strips. Arrange in a lattice pattern on the torte. Bake at 375 degrees for 35 minutes or until the pastry is crisp. Serves eight.

So much of the future lies in preserving our past.
— Peter Westbrook

RECIPE

Fondest memories from

Now is the heyday of summer. The full, warm robust middle age of the year; the earth ripe with products as well as promise.

— Daniel Grayson

Share a recipe and a memory for a special Dowry cookbook for

____

❑ *Bring this recipe to the shower*

❑ *Send your recipe to the address below and it will be entered into the Dowry Cookbook prior to the shower:*

Name: ______________________________

Address: ______________________________

Name of recipe: ______________________________

Serves: __________

Memory: ______________________________

____

____

____

Ingredients: ______________________________

____

____

____

____

____

____

____

Directions: *Preheat oven to:* __________

____

____

____

____

____

____

____

Recipe contributed by: ______________________________

For information about
The Dowry Cookbook
or other products write to:

The Dowry Cookie Co., Inc.
Attention Dowry Cookbook Dept.
P.O. Box 25091
Providence, R.I. 02905

Name ______________________________

Address ____________________________

____

City/State/Zip ______________________

____

Number of copies __________
Cost $29.95 per book __________
RI residents add $2.10 sales tax per book __________
Postage & handling $3.50 __________
Total cost __________

Make checks payable to
The Dowry Cookie Co., Inc.

Please make sure you have copied the preceding page before you use this form.

For information about
The Dowry Cookbook
or other products write to:

The Dowry Cookie Co., Inc.
Attention Dowry Cookbook Dept.
P.O. Box 25091
Providence, R.I. 02905

Name ______________________________

Address ____________________________

____

City/State/Zip ______________________

____

Number of copies __________
Cost $29.95 per book __________
RI residents add $2.10 sales tax per book __________
Postage & handling $3.50 __________
Total cost __________

Make checks payable to
The Dowry Cookie Co., Inc.

Please make sure you have copied the preceding page before you use this form.